Preface

My children, it is I, Saint Bernadette, who is speaking to you! I cannot contain my pleasure as I tell you about the Most Sweet, the Most Beautiful, and the Most Wonderful Blessed Virgin Mary, who appeared to me in 1858. Since this glorious time of my life on Earth, the Virgin Mary has never ceased to be by my side, and we have prayed together in response to every prayer heard at the Grotto of Lourdes and around the world. The Marian miracles are true, great, miraculous, and, above all, marvelous in their tenderness and love!

I love you,
Saint Bernadette

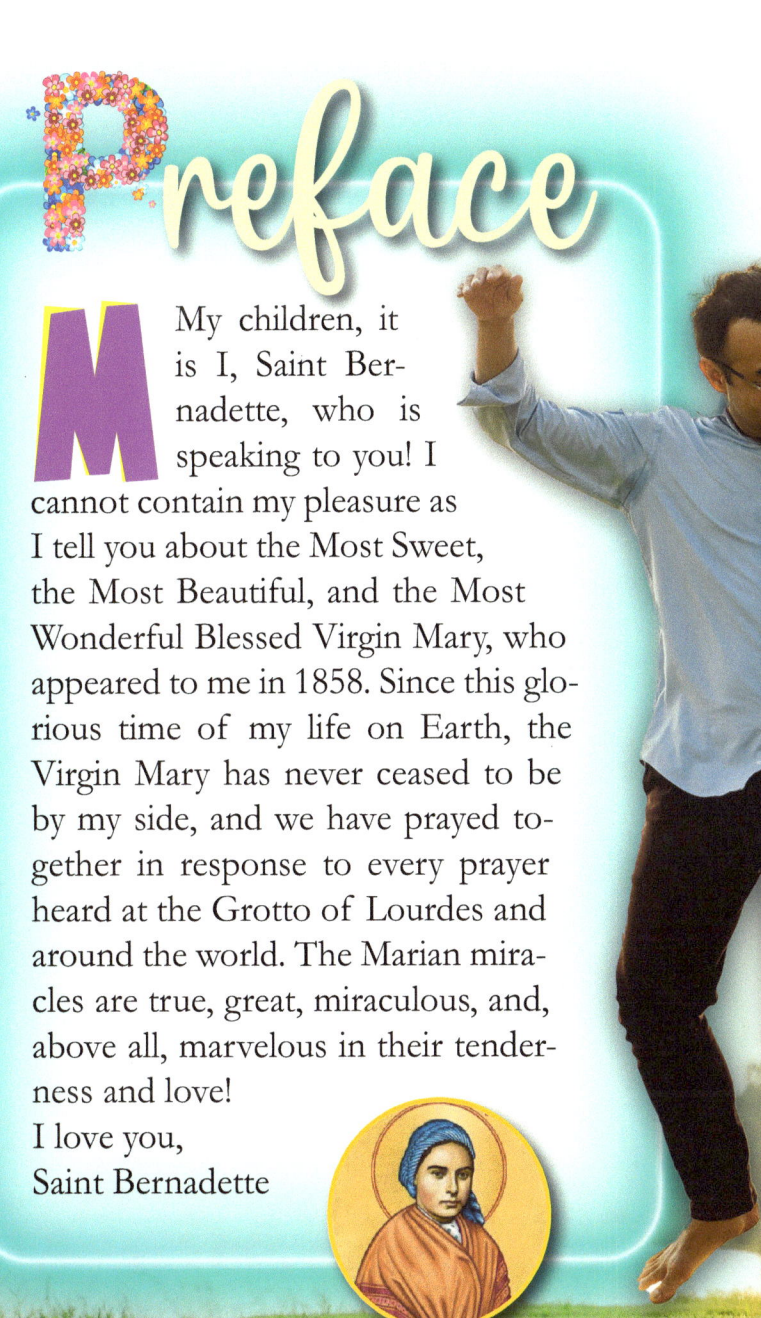

Chapter 27 — 90	Chapter 35 — 112	Chapter 44 — 133
Chapter 28 — 94	Chapter 36 — 115	Chapter 45 — 135
Chapter 20 — 95	Chapter 37 — 117	Chapter 46 — 137
Chapter 29 — 96	Chapter 38 — 119	Chapter 47 — 139
Chapter 30 — 99	Chapter 39 — 120	Chapter 48 — 140
Chapter 31 — 103	Chapter 40 — 123	Chapter 49 — 145
Chapter 32 — 106	Chapter 41 — 126	Chapter 50 — 147
Chapter 33 — 109	Chapter 42 — 128	Chapter 51 — 148
Chapter 34 — 110	Chapter 43 — 130	Afterword — 153

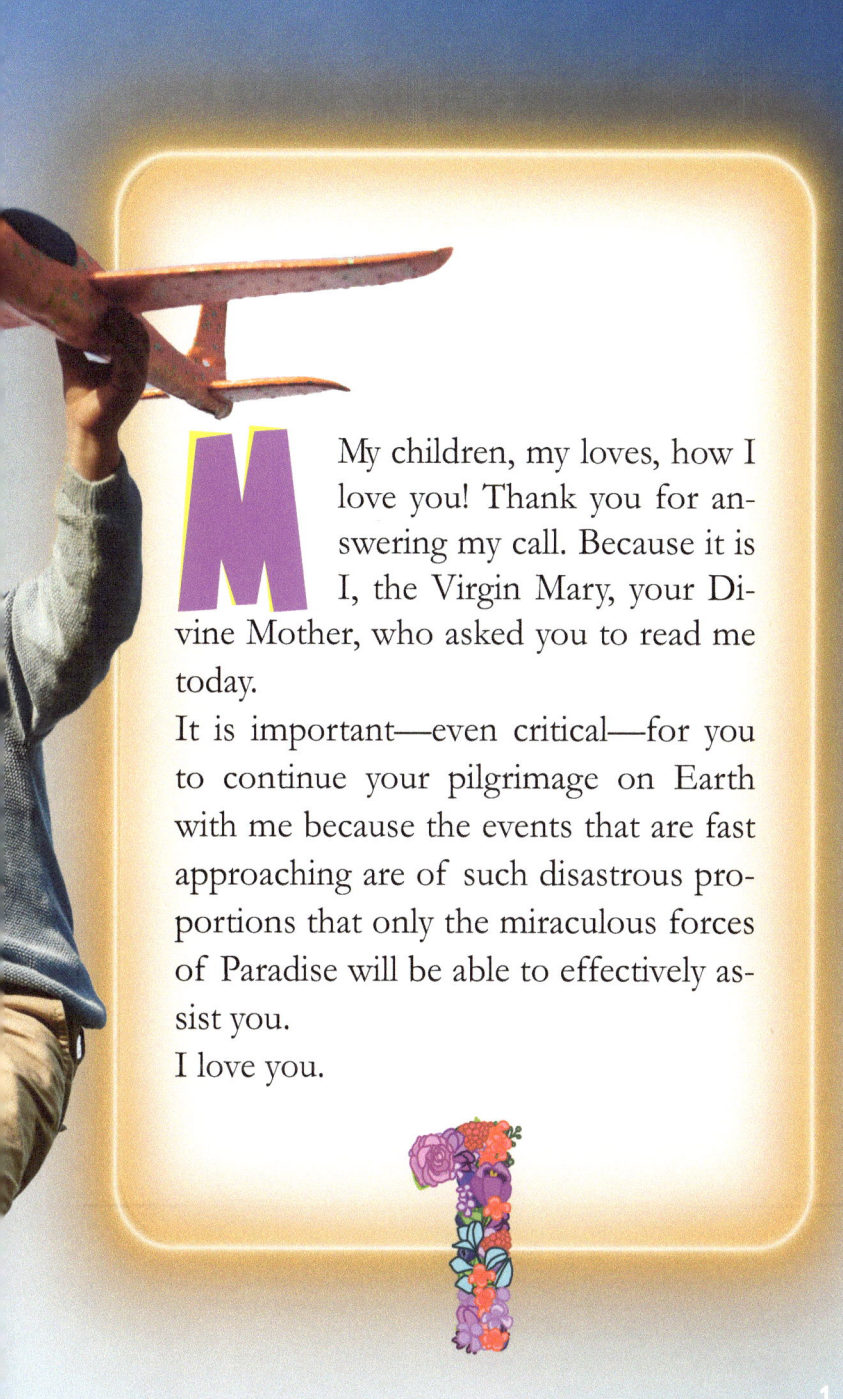

My children, my loves, how I love you! Thank you for answering my call. Because it is I, the Virgin Mary, your Divine Mother, who asked you to read me today.

It is important—even critical—for you to continue your pilgrimage on Earth with me because the events that are fast approaching are of such disastrous proportions that only the miraculous forces of Paradise will be able to effectively assist you.

I love you.

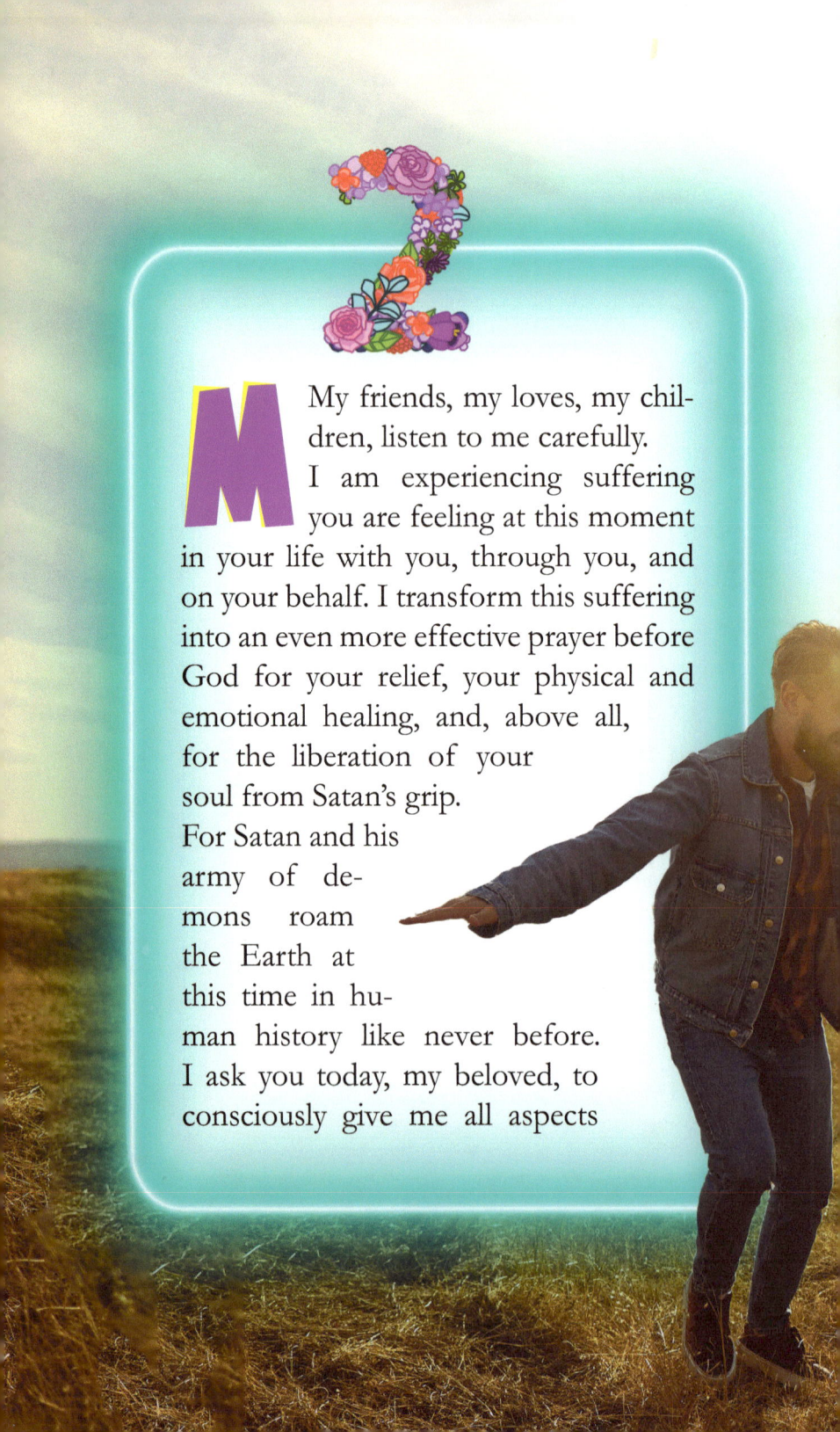

2

My friends, my loves, my children, listen to me carefully.

I am experiencing suffering you are feeling at this moment in your life with you, through you, and on your behalf. I transform this suffering into an even more effective prayer before God for your relief, your physical and emotional healing, and, above all, for the liberation of your soul from Satan's grip. For Satan and his army of demons roam the Earth at this time in human history like never before. I ask you today, my beloved, to consciously give me all aspects

of your pain and suffering.

I ask you, my child, to kneel before my effigy and to speak to me sincerely, abundantly, and above all with a profusion of tears that I know you hide in your heart.

I love you.

3

My friends, my loves, listen to me carefully.

My heart belongs to each one of you; in equal measure, each of your hearts belongs to me. This is the divine mystery of our mystical union in dimensions you would not suspect! Let me explain.

Your soul belongs to God. A part of your soul sits in your heart, and a part of your soul sits in Heaven with me, your Mother in Heaven and your Virgin Mary.

Do you see?

Your soul extends much further than you can imagine. This is why I am granted precise and detailed knowledge of your life on Earth.

Let us give glory to God for so much

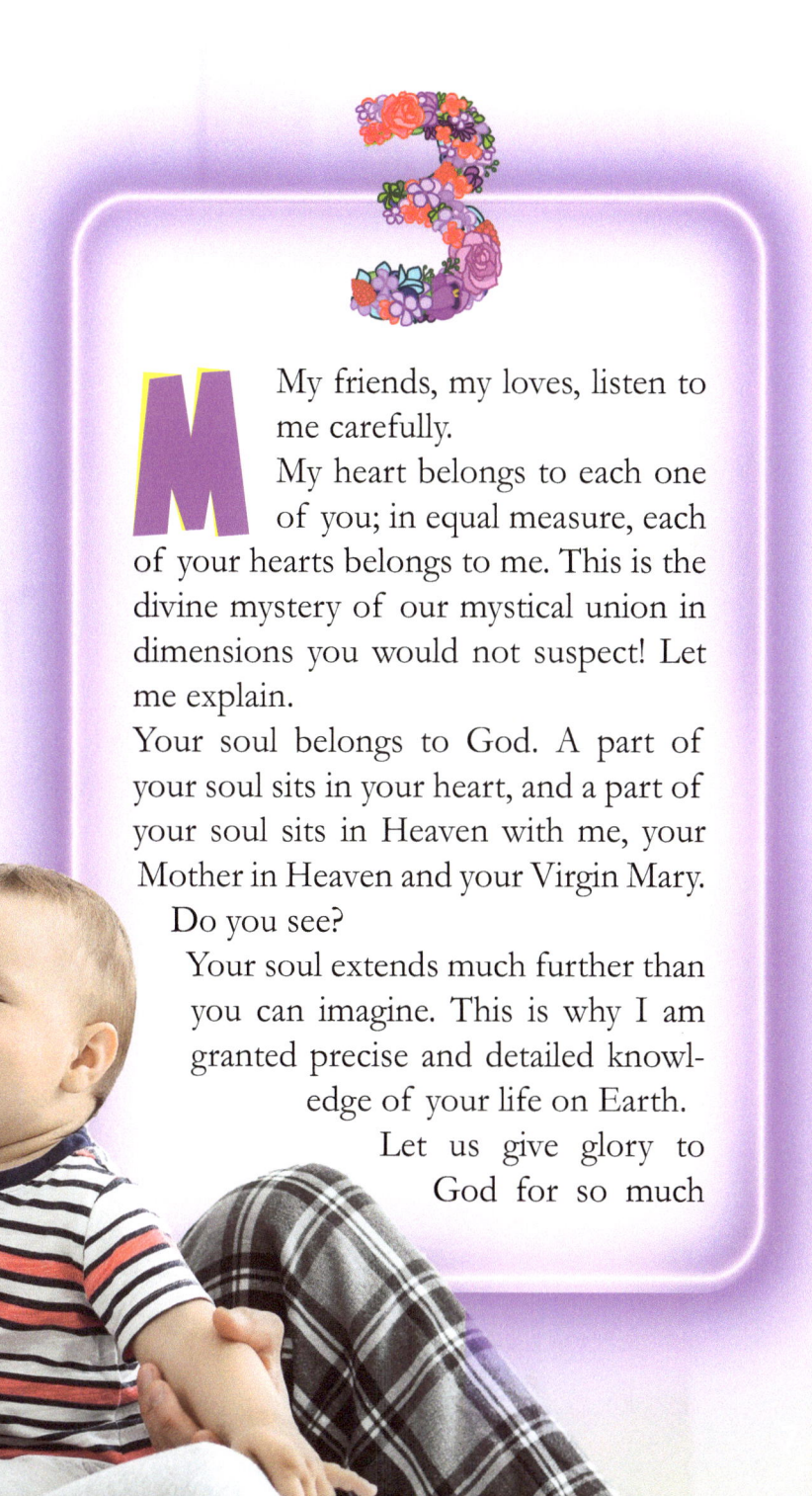

mercy on Earth upon each and every one of you because of this supernatural mystical closeness, far beyond your understanding. Therefore, strengthen your faith in Me! Amen. Alleluia!
I love you.

4

My children, hearts of my heart, I embrace you eternally. Today, I will teach you the wonderful mysteries of the physical miracles witnessed on my body-statue that you know. Indeed, I will explain to you the miraculous phenomena involving anomalies seen on my statues, such as tears of water, holy oil, and blood. I love you.

My children of my heart of glory, enter into my glory.

Today, dear children, I will teach you the mysteries of the three-dimensional planes in which you live. Know, my children, that the universe created by God is much more complex and much more refined than scientists can imagine. Indeed, there are several hundred dimensions of which you do not even suspect the existence. These dimensions are fluid for us, the inhabitants of Paradise, and they allow us to travel very quickly, to visit you as we wish, and, above all, to truly love you. I love you.

Let us give glory to God for the intricate and beautiful details of the universe that He created out of love for us. Amen! Alleluia!

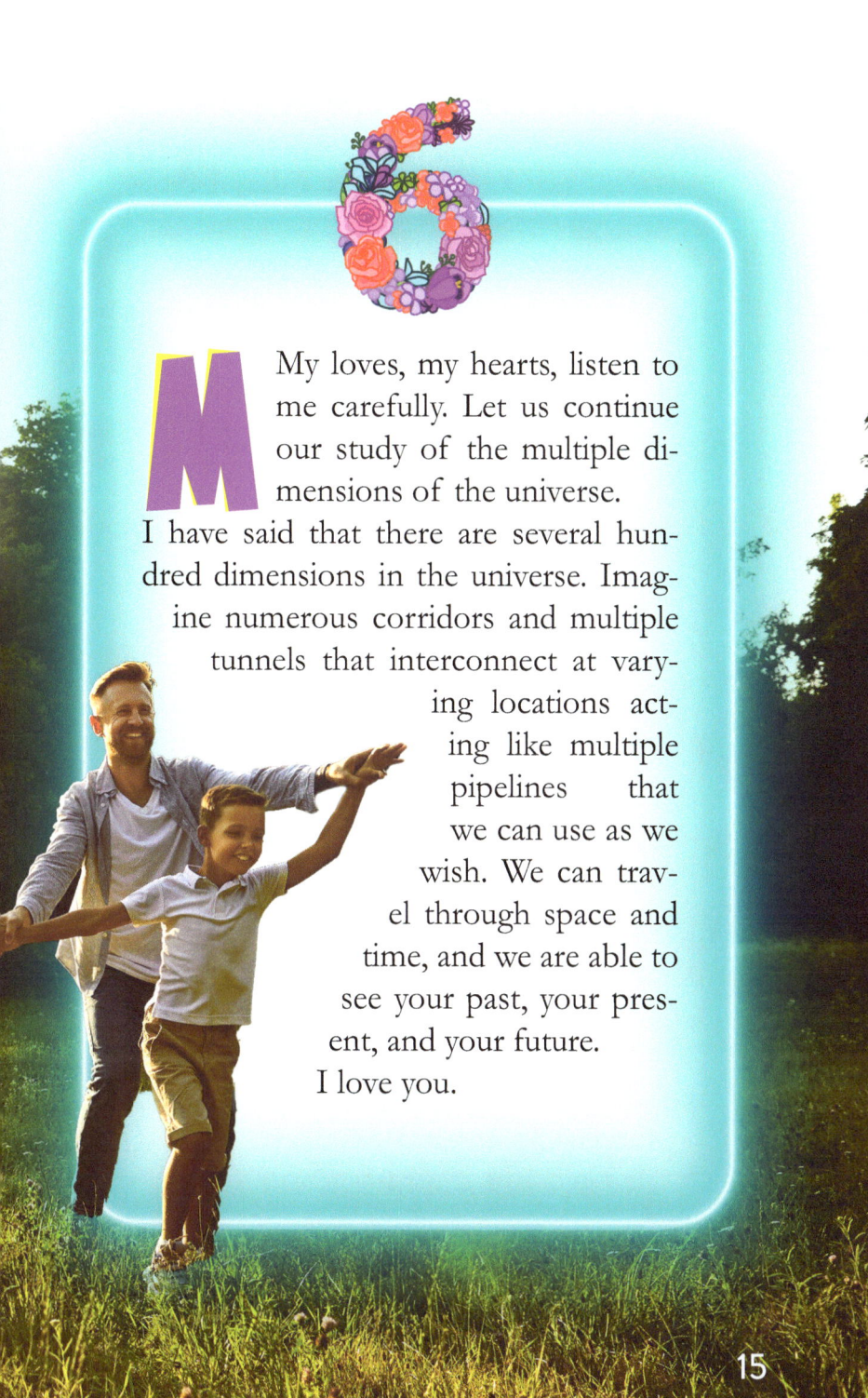

6

My loves, my hearts, listen to me carefully. Let us continue our study of the multiple dimensions of the universe.

I have said that there are several hundred dimensions in the universe. Imagine numerous corridors and multiple tunnels that interconnect at varying locations acting like multiple pipelines that we can use as we wish. We can travel through space and time, and we are able to see your past, your present, and your future.

I love you.

7

M   Dear hearts, dear loves, listen to me carefully.

Life on Earth represents only one three-dimensional aspect of the universe created by God, our Father. Indeed, the dimension in which you, and by this I mean the entire human race, live is confined in a single dimension, very heavy, very dark, and very far from Paradise.

God the Almighty Father has permitted me to make several visits. You are aware of the places of pilgrimage established all over the world in my honor and my Grace. I give thanks to God at this moment of your reading for the establishment and popularity of these places of pilgrimage dedicated to my name, and which edify my Grace, for

I am the Virgin Mary, your Divine Mother, servant of God, and Mother of the Savior. Amen! Alleluia!
I love you.

My children, my sweethearts, my life, listen to me carefully. Today, I am talking to you about the most beautiful mystery on Earth: the mystery of life itself, that is, of the source of life. By this, I mean that your life is not confined to your physical body that walks on the Earth's crust. No! The life that inhabits you, that you interpret to the heart that beats in your chest, is life only—far from that! The life that animates you is derived from the Fire of the Central Sun, which was created at the very beginning of Genesis. This flow of life crosses hundreds and hundreds of dimensions before stopping in your physical body—this temporary envelope on Earth. I love you.

My beloved children, listen to me carefully.

The miraculous apparition of Our Lady of Lourdes to the unique eyes of Saint Bernadette Soubirous was the most marvelous of all Marian apparitions!

Indeed, the entire Paradise prayed hard so that God Himself would agree to implement this prodigious phenomenon of nature on Earth, for the miraculous water of Lourdes truly takes its source in Paradise with us. Be assured, dear children of my Grace, that the primordial source of the miraculous water of Lourdes that is—in fact—located in Paradise is constantly visited and

blessed by countless Angels, the Saints in Paradise, pure souls, and of course by myself, your Divine Mother, the Blessed Virgin Mary. This wonderful water emits an extraordinary energetic vibration that cannot be measured by your modern scientific methods.

Alleluia! Alleluia! Alleluia! Blessed is he who firmly believes in the miraculous properties of the Eternal Water of Lourdes, for Paradise has already opened to him. Amen. Alleluia!

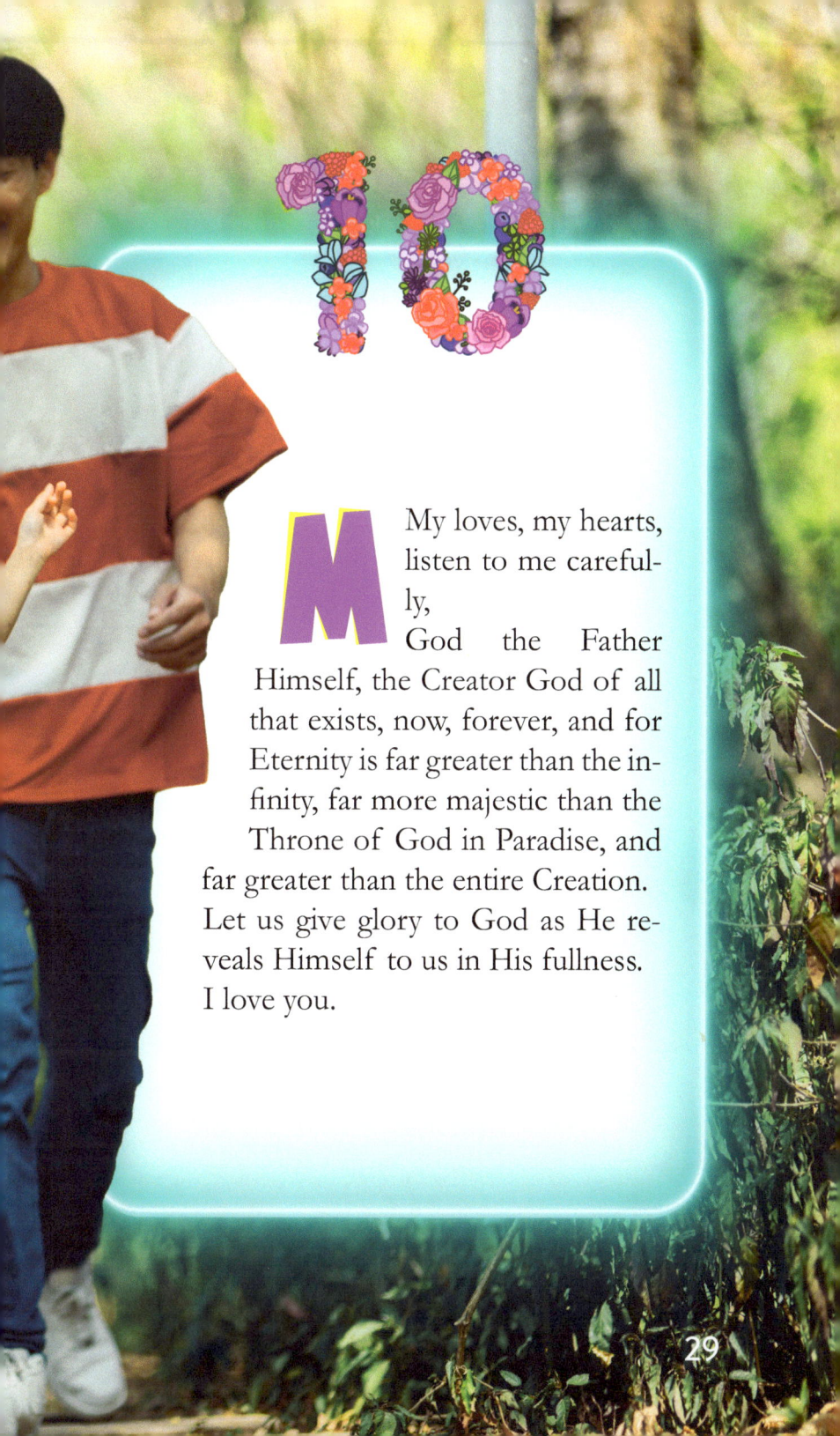

10

My loves, my hearts, listen to me carefully,

God the Father Himself, the Creator God of all that exists, now, forever, and for Eternity is far greater than the infinity, far more majestic than the Throne of God in Paradise, and far greater than the entire Creation. Let us give glory to God as He reveals Himself to us in His fullness. I love you.

11

Dear soul who inhabits my heart for eternity.

I ask you, dear little fragile creature in this world of darkness, to admire, to love, and to adore the Cross of our Savior all, my Son Jesus Christ, our Lord, forever and ever. This Cross contains the wonders of redemption and the Paschal mysteries so precious for the salvation of your soul.

I love you.

12

My children of love, listen to me carefully.

The apparition of the Universal Virgin Mary at Fatima filled me with immense joy! My apparition made it possible to deliver humanity from war. The Virgin Mary offered many messages of comfort and the edification of the soul. Above all, the Virgin Mary brought down to Earth a wonderful miracle directly from Paradise.

Indeed, the Miracle of the Sun materialized because the entire

Paradise was transported, for a very brief moment, to Earth by virtue of an extraordinary transfer of energy emanating from the Central Sun. This is because Paradise is truly located deep within the physical sun that you see every day in the sky, which warms you, illuminates you, and, above all, graces you.

Amen! Alleluia!

I love you.

The Miracle of the Sun

Fatima Sanctuary in Portugal, - Our Lady of Fátima marian shrine square

13

My children of love, listen to me carefully.

As I am gentle and good, it is possible for you to love me; however, this love is childish and easy. The greatness of your true love is measured through the pain and suffering of your life. Love me, your mother in Heaven, in the midst of the tragic trials that are beyond your immediate control and that force you to pray,

to pray to God, Jesus, the Saints in Paradise, and myself, the Most Blessed Virgin Mary, your Divine Mother.

This is the true love that you will live in your heart by decision of the Father. For true love for the Most Blessed Virgin Mary, your Divine Mother, is determinant especially at the moment of the passage that is death. I love you.

14

My children, my loves, listen to me carefully.

It is by the Grace of God, the Almighty Father, the Universal Divine Mother that I am able to cross the heavy dimensions of your planet in order to manifest my presence, my power and, above all, my Love.

I say unto you, I say unto you verily: The blue rays of my presence on Earth are manifested through the statues made in my likeness according to the precise and effective will of God. Today, we will begin our study of Marian miracles.

I love you.

15

My loves of the whole Earth, listen to me carefully.

The appearance of the Universal Virgin Mary to San Juan Diego in Mexico appealed to me much more than other Marian miracles not only because Juan was a man of good will and pure and whose heart was ready for this mystical encounter with his divine mother, but because of the miraculous tilma.

Know, my children, that this tilma of love was conceived, drawn, and produced in Paradise by

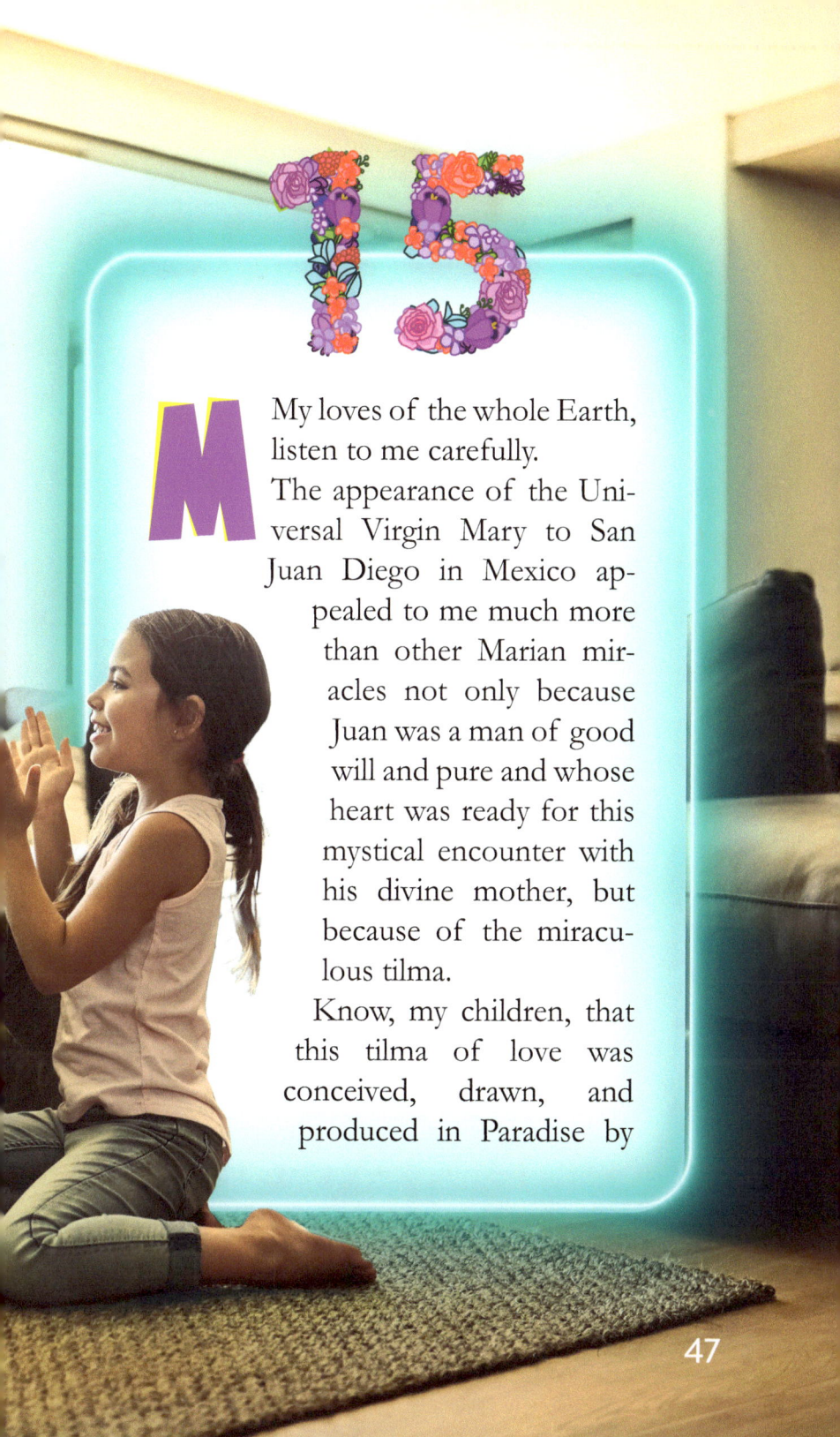

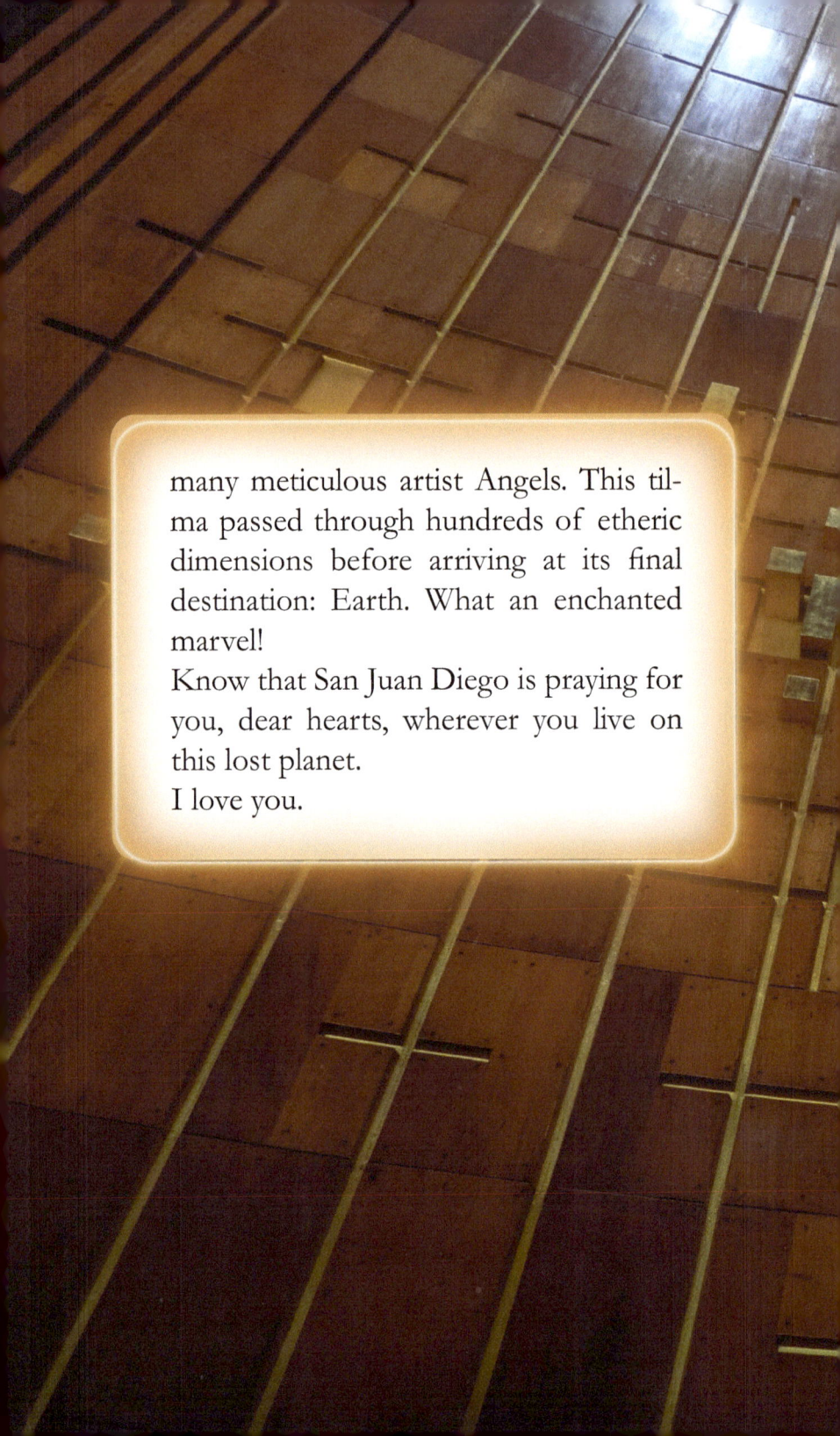

many meticulous artist Angels. This tilma passed through hundreds of etheric dimensions before arriving at its final destination: Earth. What an enchanted marvel!

Know that San Juan Diego is praying for you, dear hearts, wherever you live on this lost planet.

I love you.

MEXICO CITY, MEXICO: Tourists and locals visit Basilica of Our Lady of Guadalupe in Mexico City

Mexico City, Mexico, historical landmark Basilica of Our Lady of Guadalupe and Mexico City

My little children in my arms, listen to me carefully.

There exists a mystical life that you may not suspect that is far beyond your concept of a statue made in my likeness, which is inert and inorganic. Indeed, the Father, in all his Divine Mercy allows me to impregnate my Grace, my power, my maternal presence, and above all, my Love, throughout, inside, outside, from one side to the other, and from bottom to top of each statue made in my likeness, small and large, and this throughout the entire Earth. I thank God for that wonderful miracle.

I love you.

17

My little hearts in my hands of Mother, listen to me carefully.

When you enter your parish church today, pay close attention to my statues made in my likeness. Look closely at the eyes of Mary, of myself, of your Heavenly Mother. In fact, I ask you to focus all of your consciousness on my physical eyes. Verily, verily I say unto you, my eyes will take on a surreal and supernatural organic life. For I truly inhabit every statue made in my likeness locat-

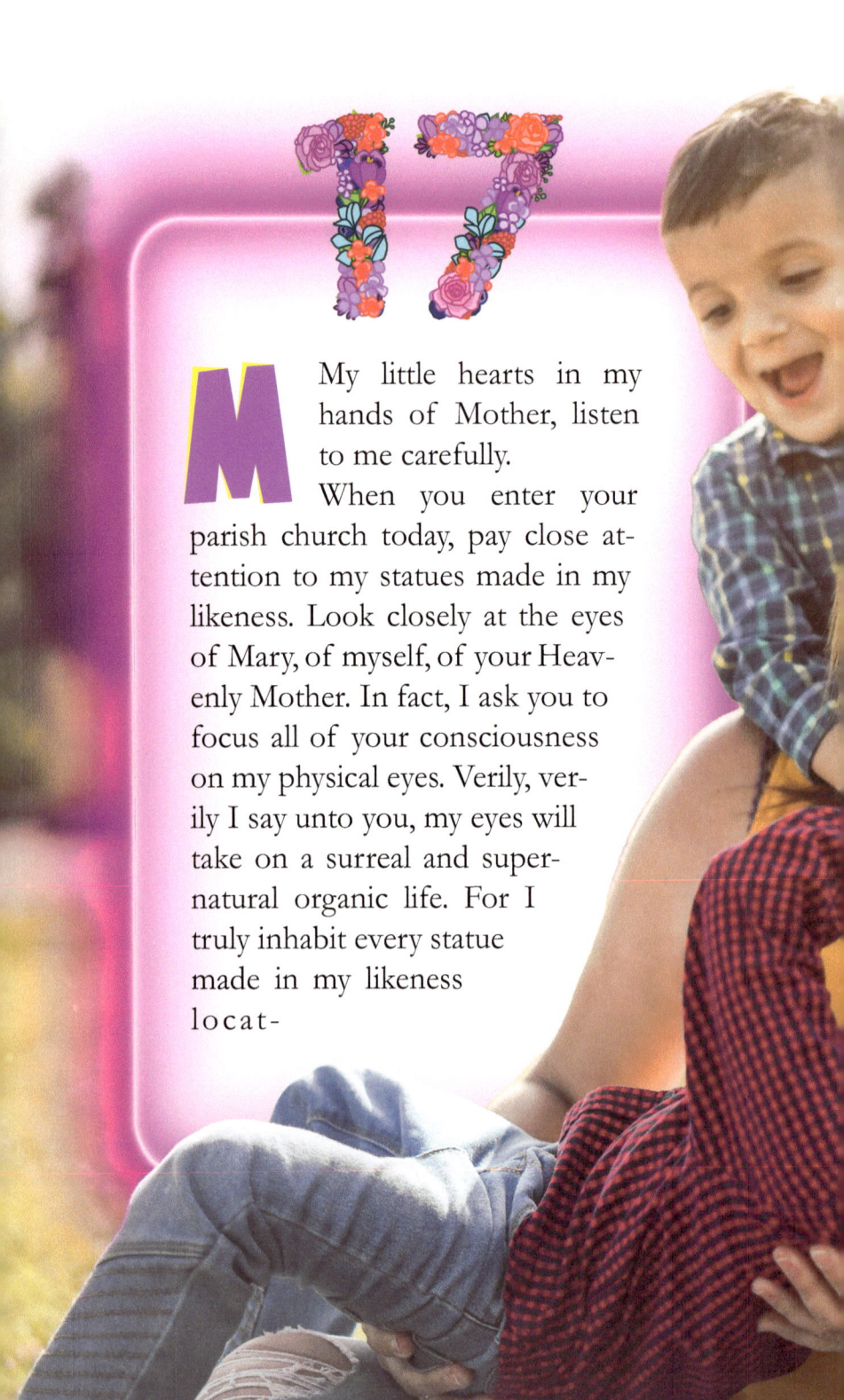

ed everywhere on Earth, simultaneously, equally, eternally, completely, and, above all, with love and power. Let us give glory to God for this sweet miracle He has allowed. I love you.

18

My hearts, my beloved, listen to me carefully.

My appearance in Međugorje was the culmination of intense prayers on the part of the inhabitants of Paradise. Indeed, the community of the inhabitants of Paradise greatly desired hat multiple Marian apparitions manifest before several children simultaneously in order to increase the credibility of the divine message given.

The Marian apparitions in Međugorje continue to manifest themselves and will never stop, for God Himself has decided so. I thank God for granting so much mercy on your souls.

I love you.

View of Saint James Church in Medjugorje, destination of pilgrims

19

Dear souls and hearts of my heart, listen to me carefully.

I will explain to you the nature of the tears seen on my statues or images made in my likeness. These tears symbolize sorrow, compassion, and the transparency of the suffering soul. Above all, however, these tears are projected from the depths of my mystical and universal soul manifested to you. In other words, the tears on my statues or images made in my likeness reach your physical and very heavy dimension after having traveled through hundreds of etheric dimensions that you do not know. I love you.

Painting Icon of the Virgin Mary with Infant Jesus Shed Watery Tears, Chicago (2019)

A caretaker who works at Holy Trinity Greek Orthodox Church in Belmont Central witnessed the miracle. The church has not commented. This miracle took place the week prior to the church being sold off due to a foreclosure.

Weeping Mary and Infant Jesus, Serbia (2024)

Local scientists have attempted to determine the exact chemical composition of the oil, but they have been unable to do so. It is felt to be a non-terrestrial creation. The chemical composition resembles olive oil, although not quite exactly. When wiped off, the oil flows again from that place that is from nowhere, and yet it is there. The Church Commission continues to monitor this phenomenon.

20

My hearts, my joy, my delights, listen to me carefully.

The tears on the statues made in my likeness can be composed of water, oil, or blood. In the next chapters, I explain each of the manifestations in detail. Let us thank God for the wonderful exchange of love here and now! I love you.

21

My loves of love, listen to me carefully.

We continue our study of the marvelous tears that occasionally appear on the statues made in my likeness. Tears of water refer to baptismal water. Tears of oil signify a more organic penetration through my holy humanity. Tears of blood signify my supreme cosmic presence in this likeness and manifestation of my holy soul united with my holy body. I love you.

Virgin Mary Statue Cries Tears of Blood, Carmiano, Lecce, Italy (2020)

This miracle is still under investigation. The tears appeared on one side only.

Virgin Mary Statue Crying Tears of Blood, Sacramento, California (2005)

A red trail can be seen from the side of the statue's left eye to about halfway down the robe of concrete. The diocese of Sacramento has not commented.

22

My children of greatest love, listen to me carefully.

Tears of water are natural and flow from my two eyes in a symmetrical, identical manner, and with the same exact abundance. Examine the photos of the tears on my statue that froze over the winter. This powerful and romantic phenomenon is linked to my emotions of compassion, sadness, and, in particular, intense grief. I love you.

Our Lady of Akita, Yuzawadai, Japan (1973)

Our Lady of Akita is a title of the Blessed Virgin Mary associated with Marian apparitions that Sister Agnes Katsuko Sasagawa reported in 1973 in Yuzawadai, Japan. Her deafness was subsequently healed.

The Miraculous Weeping Statue of the Virgin Mary, Syracuse, Italy (1953)

An analysis of the tears revealed that they were human. This miracle has been approved by local bishops.

23

My children under my blue mantle, listen to me carefully. I explain to you today the tears of oil that were demonstrated on my likeness- body. These tears are unique in that they are connected to my spiritual and cosmic nature and reveal the significant depth of the Marian miraculous phenomenon. The manifestation of tears of oil has its origin in the deep, subtle, refined, and very high dimensions that originate in Paradise. This explains the sweet and floral fragrance that accompanies them. I love you.

Virgin Mary Statue is Crying tears, El Canal, Colima, Mexico (2023)

A statue located in a Catholic church in the town of El Canal, Colima, was recorded showing what looks like tears seeping out of the Virgin Mary's eyes. This miracle is still under investigation by the Catholic church.

Weeping Virgin Mary Statue, Hobbs, NM (2023)

Experts analyzed the substance and concluded it was olive oil mixed with perfume, similar in composition to chrism, the holy anointment balm often used in Christian rites such as baptism. However, local church authorities reportedly could not establish where the oil was coming from. This miracle is still under analysis by the Catholic church.

24

My friends of joy, listen to me carefully.

Tears of blood represent an extremely intimate manifestation of the Universal Virgin Mary. Tears of blood originate from Passion of my Son Jesus, our Savior, and my union with Him, my Jesus, my Savior, my Son and my God, in the cosmic mysteries of redemption and manifested mercy. The vibrations linked to these manifestations are so powerful that they are comparable to those of the day of the crucifixion of my beloved Son two thousand years ago. I love you.

Mary's Statue Shedding Tears of Blood in Ghaziabad, India (2012)

On Saturday 14 July 2012, in Ghaziabad, Uttar Pradesh, India, a statue of Mary, brought a few months before from St. Paul's Centre, New Delhi, shed tears of blood. The bleeding occurred four times on three consecutive days from July 14, 2012.

Weeping Virgin Mary Sheds Tears of Blood, Caracas, Venezuela (2003)

A statue of the Virgin Mary weeping a red liquid that Venezuelans say is blood was witnessed on March 25, 2003 in Caracas, Venezuela. The local church did not comment.

My beloved children of my heart, listen to me carefully. Perhaps there are incidents in your life that have made you confused and sad. I ask you today, dear heart of my heart, to take a small house statuette of the Virgin Mary, your Divine Mother, myself who is speaking to you at this moment, and to place this statuette very close to you, on the kitchen table, at your bedside, or at your work desk. Take this statuette often in your hands, kiss it, love it, and be assured that I, your Divine Mother, receives precisely and physically all this tenderness and all this love for me and that your devotion addresses to me. I love you.

26

My beloveds of my glorified heart, listen to me carefully,

The tears of water, blood, or oil that escape from my eyes through images and statues made in my likeness are significant on all levels. These tears are a sign of my mystical presence inside this image or statue. They symbolize my pain, my sadness,

Weeping Madonna, Hempstead, New York (1960)

A vintage picture of Madonna and Child on table, surrounded by flowers and candles, in a home in Hempstead, New York. Madonna has tears on her face. Catholic church leaders have witnessed and reported the miracle.

and, above all, the intensity of my emotions of compassion. This is a sign of the Father's power and love for all his children. This is a sign that I am speaking to you, my beloved child. I love you.

27

My friends, my loves, listen to me carefully.

Life with me is well-hidden deep in my bosom, beneath my mantle of blue suns, brings blessing, miracles, wisdom, and, above all, the profound peace of Paradise. Life with me is a life that takes place partly in Heaven and partly here on this

Our Lady of Zeitoun, Cairo, Egypt (1968))

The visions of the Most Blessed Virgin Mary occurring in multiple apparitions have been witnessed by thousands of people above a church in Cairo, Egypt.

decaying Earth. This is why the Marian apparitions and miraculous appearances are direct and tangible manifestations of Paradise on Earth, through the agency of the Holy Spirit, God the Holy Spirit. I love you.

28

My beautiful souls under my blue mantle, listen to me carefully.

Marian miracles are not derived from my personal will, although my will is divine, cosmic, generous and merciful. Indeed, each documented or undocumented Marian miracle on Earth is the direct result of the decision of the Absolute Father, Abba Father, who is exclusively sovereign over each miraculous phenomenon. Let us give thanks to God for offering so much mercy to humanity. I love you.

29

My beloved children both small and big, listen to me carefully.

Marian miracles represent God's mercy in its profound origin. Indeed, I cannot manifest myself to the whole world, either to an individual or globally, unless God the Almighty Father grants my exclusive and urgent request. In other words, permission to manifest myself to you, regardless of the type of manifestation and location in the world, is primarily, exclusively, and sovereignly God's decision. I thank God for bestowing so much mercy on my beloved children. I love you.

30

Hearts of my caresses, listen to me well.

Miraculous Marian manifestations unfold like this: God first grants me His approval. Then, I decide on the geographical location of my divine manifestation over the world. I then choose the church and the statue. Subsequently, I invest all my Marian Grace through this statue. Shortly, and with the assistance of Angels, my Marian Grace will manifest itself, predominantly with tears of water, oil, or blood, which represent different depths and manifestations of my Grace. Let us give thanks to God for providing so much mercy in your life. I love you.

A Statue of the Virgin Mary in a House in Fresno Appears to be Weeping Tears of Water, Fresno, California (2016)

The family who owns the statue calls it a miracle and says that it has been happening for a few months. Tears seem to well up in her right eye and stream down her face to her chin. The owner of the house collects the tears in a glass and shares them with those who find their way to the home. Priests of the diocese confirm that this is a miracle.

31

My little hearts, listen to me carefully. No one can see me in all my deeply hidden, living, and vibrant splendor through a statue made in my likeness unless your soul is awakened to me. Thus, I wish to teach you today that the greatness and depth of your love for me, your Divine Mother, the Virgin Mary, opens your eyes to the mystical vision of my gracious presence here. Few souls have obtained these graces on Earth. Marie-Josée, my beloved

daughter, is among these few.
Blessed be my beautiful daughter Marie-Josée, who takes down this dictation at this moment as I speak to her, and who gives herself completely to her difficult mission on Earth. I love you.

32

My children of my sacred heart, listen to me carefully.

There remain spiritual and miraculous Marian manifestations resulting from divine mercy that are far beyond the Marian manifestations at the physical level through statues made in my likeness. These miracles are numerous and take place in your hearts, your bodies, your families and friends, but, above all, in your individual souls, for I am your Divine Mother, your Virgin Mary. At an individual and personal level, my love for you is limitless. I love you.

33

My beloved children of my adorable heart, listen to me carefully.

A gentle word from you towards me is more meritorious, miraculous, precious and, above all, intimate with me than you can imagine. I am closer to you than your own family, your spouse, your children, and your friends. In fact, I am closer to you and more intimate with you than your own skin! I love you.

My little hearts of my heart, listen to me carefully.

Marian miracles are the subject of intense public attention on Earth for good reason. The love that all my children have for me is part of God's plan of salvation. Rest assured, dear hearts of my heart, that celebrations in Heaven are constantly organized and take place with rejoicing that is unparalleled on Earth, for the entirety of Paradise is attentive and constantly informed of the events unfolding on Earth, in particular the Marian miracles and other miracles whose intercessions are carried out by the Saints in Paradise. I love you.

35

My beloved children of love, listen to me carefully. The Kingdom of Heaven is far greater than you can imagine. The concentrations of pure souls are distributed everywhere and according to family trees, collective tribes, and climatic differences. Indeed, humans continue to live their lives in Heaven in a landscape and climatic environment like that on Earth. Tropical, sub-tropical, continental, and arctic climates are found here, and pure souls ceaselessly celebrate this ineffable and unexpected grace.
I love you.

My children of love, listen to me carefully.

Perhaps you have abandoned the practice of reciting the rosary? Perhaps your prayers have lost the burning fire of motivation and faith? Today, dear little hearts, dear little souls, make a radical inner decision and give me your commandment for this day. Ask for my intercession several times throughout the day and my influence on you will be multiplied. In addition, carry with you in your pocket and close to your body your rosary, a small statuette made in my likeness, or a pious image. The vibrations associated with my physical presence near your body are much more powerful than you can imagine. I love you.

37

MLove of my life in Paradise, listen to me carefully.

My protection and love are fundamental to your emotional, spiritual, and physical balance. My glorious and fantastic intercession manifests itself in your life on several levels in an extremely refined and subtle way, but also in a directly physical and organic way—that is to say, in your human flesh. The powers of the Blessed Virgin Mary extend across hundreds of dimensions that you do not suspect but are real and dynamic. I love you.

Hearts of my heart, souls of my soul, listen to me carefully.

Today, I want to see your heart belong to me completely, perfectly, simply, and irreversibly. Pray this prayer and say out loud: "My dear Divine Mother, my personal Virgin Mary, I love you with all my heart, with all my soul, with all my strength, and I ask you to take me into your mother's arms, here and now, and not to distance yourself from me all the days of my life, especially at the moment of the passage that is death so that your presence, your love, and your power opens the gates of Paradise for my soul for eternity. Virgin Mary, I love you!

39

My loves of the whole Earth, listen to me carefully.

Far beyond your daily life exists a spiritual life that unfolds in the intimacy of your heart with me, exclusively, the Virgin Mary, Your Sweet Divine Mother. Indeed, I occupy an important part of your heart, and your relationship with me is played out here in your heart. This is where we talk to each other, pray together, say our rosary together daily, cry together, and above all, love each other.
I love you.

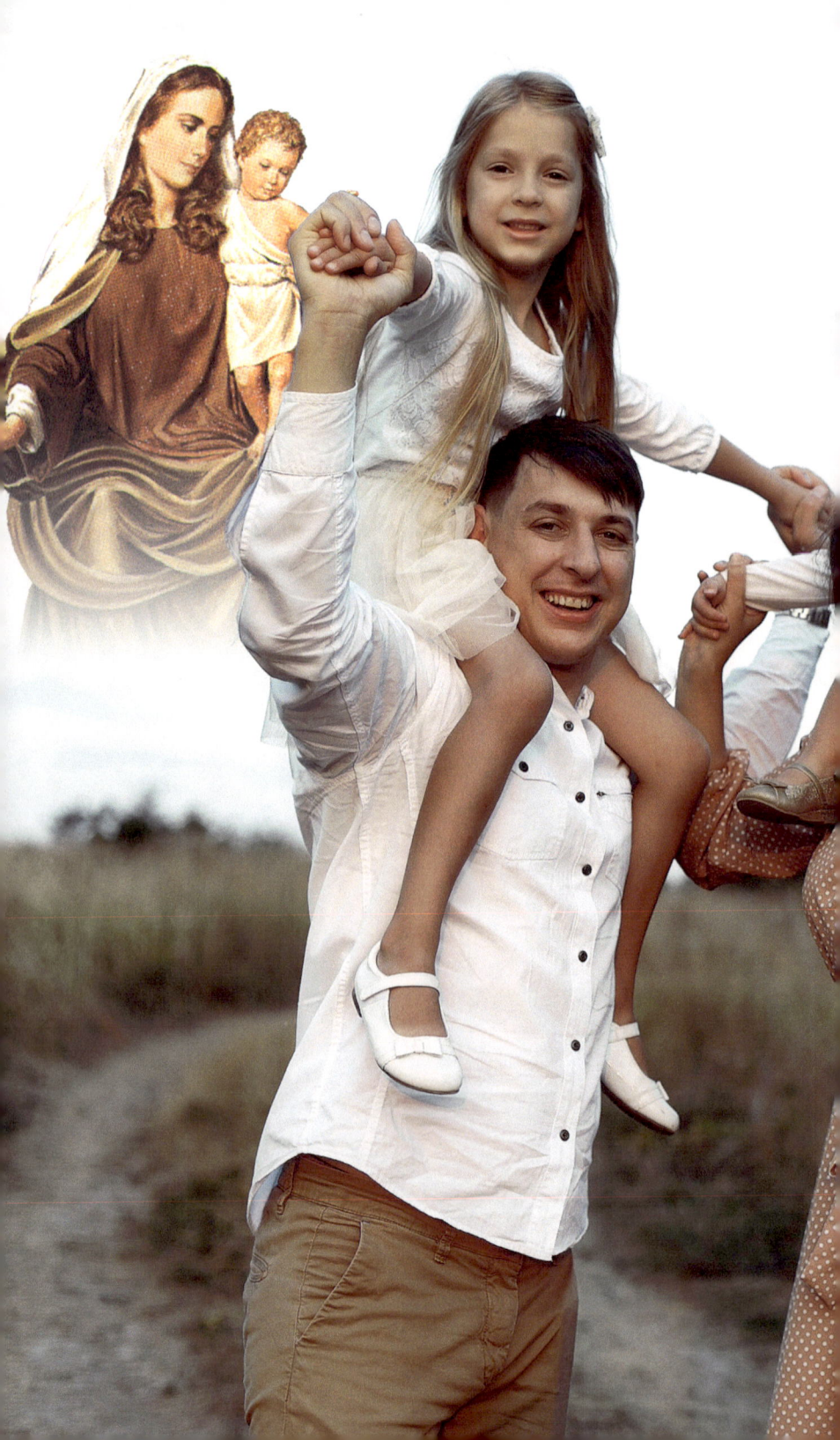

40

My grown children in my mother's arms, listen to me carefully.

It is impossible for me to omit an important teaching in relation to the day of the Great Judgment. This day has already been determined by God and is advancing with great stride. It will be a day of infinite glory for the servants of Jesus, of myself, the Virgin Mary, of the Angels, of Abba Father, and of the Saints of Paradise. This day will be a day of infinite sorrow for

the enemies of the truth contained in all the holy and sacred books that have been distributed throughout the world since the beginning of the history of humanity including the Bible, the Quran, the Torah, and other publications in which God the Father has revealed Himself to us. I love you.

41

My friends, my loves, listen to me carefully. The doors of my heart are always open, day and night, from second to second, from emotion to emotion, and this now and for eternity. Speak to me, love me, cry with me, laugh with me, and above all, pray with me!
I love you.

42

My children of the whole Earth, listen to me carefully. My mother's heart cannot accept the loss of any of my children. This is why I make divine, miraculous, cosmic and, above all, magnetic efforts in your life in order to attract you to me, to keep you under my mantle of blue suns, to make us inseparable, and, above all, to love each other without limit and without condition. Our magnetic bond is essential to successfully opening the doors of Paradise at the time of the passage that is death.

I love you.

43

My friends, my loves, listen to me carefully.

Today, I explain to you the powers hidden in my mantle of blue suns, which extends to the infinity of this creation. My mantle represents a complete, blue, and unique etheric dimension of this creation designed by God our Creator.

My mantle, therefore, extends, joins, and is fused with the gates of Paradise. Because of this incomparable and cosmic miracle, I am capable of assisting your soul as it enters Heaven through these very gates. Do you see? The gates of Paradise are a continuum of my blue mantle and vice versa.

I love you.

44

My heart and my life, listen to me carefully.

Be clear in your mind and in your heart that God the Almighty Father exercises exclusive control of the judgment bestowed upon a soul and its entry into Heaven. My cosmic and miraculous assistance softens the Heart of the Father, and my tears, prayers and supplications are heard and absorbed in Him.

Abba Father is an almighty, all-loving, all-compassionate, and, above all, all-merciful God. I love you.

My loves from all over the world, listen to me carefully.

Why do you get sad or overwhelmed, and why do you want to change everything in your life at times of minor annoyance or moral/family battles of some kind?

Pray to me, your Virgin Mary, your Divine Mother. Then, pray to me again!

In response to your prayers, my own prayers and supplications have been deposited directly in the Heart of Abba Father and are sufficient such that the Father will show you mercy on you and grant you your dream solution that is far beyond your hopes.

I love you.

46

Hearts of my heart, friends of my Grace, listen to me carefully.

Remember that you need to pray to me and say your rosary every day. This affirmation from me today must be incorporated into your daily routine in a rigorous and disciplined manner alongside the other obligations of the Catholic religion. Imagine each rosary recited with me as a decisive step towards Paradise that is made through my precious and miraculous help.

I love you.

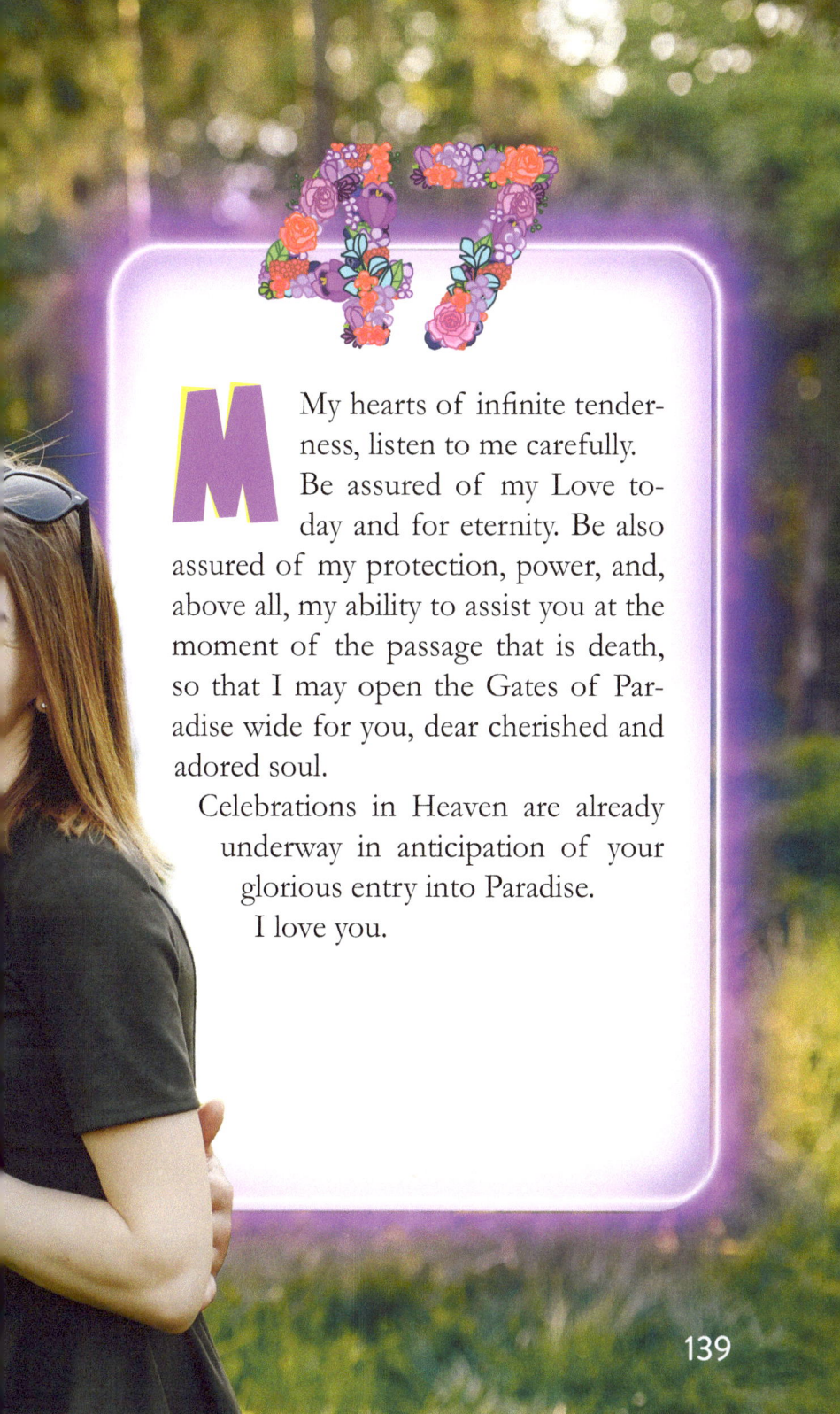

47

My hearts of infinite tenderness, listen to me carefully.

Be assured of my Love today and for eternity. Be also assured of my protection, power, and, above all, my ability to assist you at the moment of the passage that is death, so that I may open the Gates of Paradise wide for you, dear cherished and adored soul.

Celebrations in Heaven are already underway in anticipation of your glorious entry into Paradise.

I love you.

Dear little heart in my hands, listen to me carefully.

What to do when helplessness overcomes you? Take your rosary in your hands and immediately pray with me, your Heavenly Mother, the Virgin Mary, Mother of the Savior, your Divine Mother.

Statue Of Virgin Mary Weeps Oil In Tarshiha, Northern Israel (2020)

A Christian family from Tarshiha, close to the border with Lebanon, says the statue is "covered with oil" and that the phenomenon is a miracle. The local church has investigated this claim.

My presence in your heart is constant and powerful, and my comfort is immediate. Above all, the remedy for the problems encountered will be delivered simultaneously as you pray.
I love you.

49

My loves, my hearts, listen to me carefully.

Your rosary is more precious than all the gold on Earth. Hold it close to you, embrace it, caress it, and honor it. This rosary is in continuum with my Heart of Divine Mother, which is cosmic, transcendent, powerful, and derived from the Original Fire of Creation, which was present at the time of Genesis, the Cradle of Creation.

I love you.

My little ones in my arms, listen to me carefully.

Our Mother–child union cannot be qualified from your vantage point. However, the value of our relationship is the most important aspect in the Eyes of God, for our union is emotional, spiritual, loving and, above all, supernatural and is absorbed, transformed, and edified in the Heart of Abba Father, like a pearl of great cosmic value.

I love you.

51

My loves of love, my hearts, my children, listen to me carefully.

I have reached the end of this presentation explaining the manifestation of Marian miracles.

I most desire, dear heart of my heart, dear love of love, to see your heart leap with joy immediately when you see my image, hear my name, and say your rosary, particularly mo-

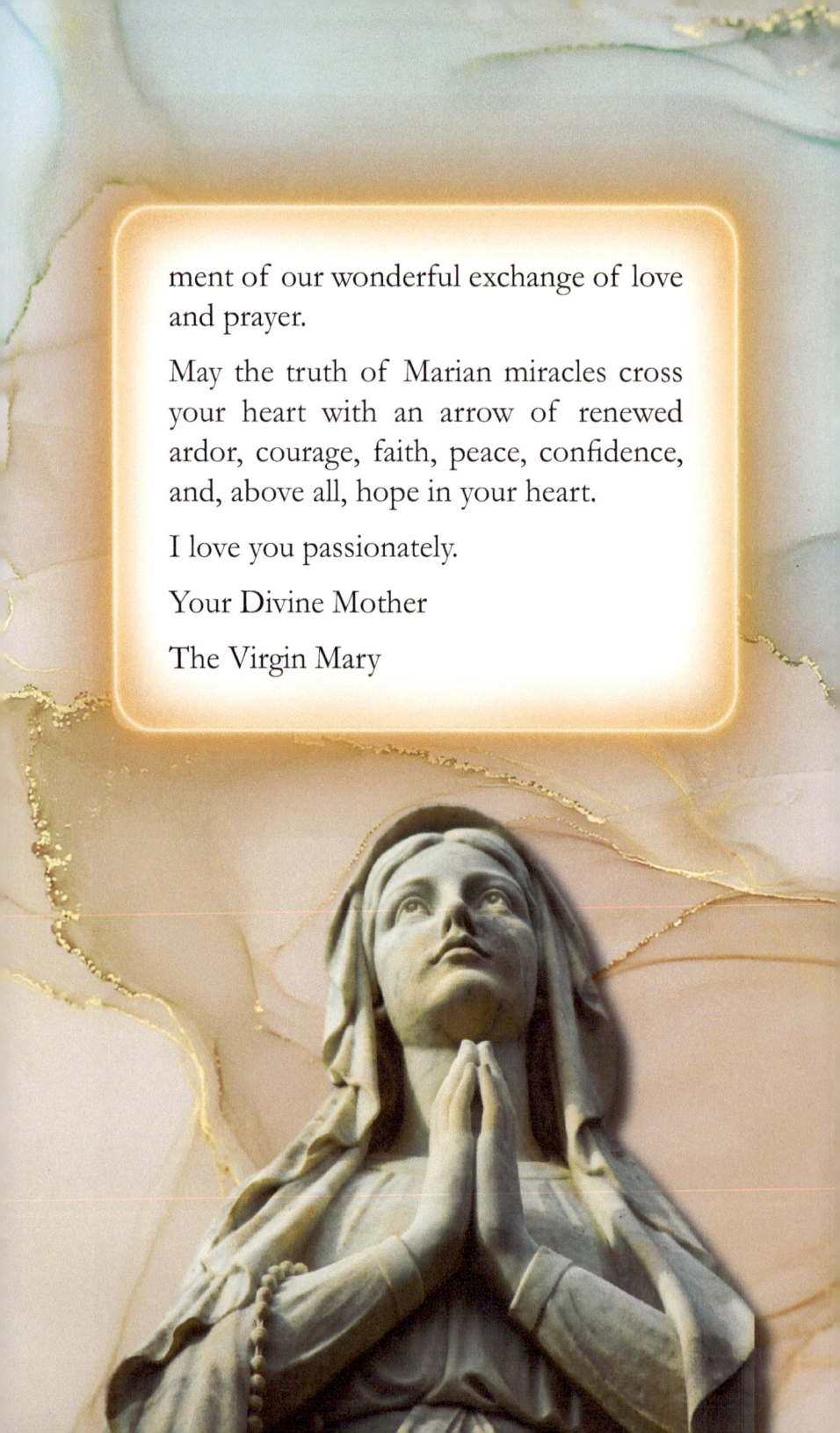

ment of our wonderful exchange of love and prayer.

May the truth of Marian miracles cross your heart with an arrow of renewed ardor, courage, faith, peace, confidence, and, above all, hope in your heart.

I love you passionately.

Your Divine Mother

The Virgin Mary

Statue of the Virgin Mary Sheds Tears of Blood, Floridablanca, Columbia (2016)

Hundreds of overjoyed pilgrims flock to a statue of the Virgin Mary believed to be crying a single tear of blood. There is a street statue in front before which the faithful of a poor neighborhood pray daily. The local church has not commented.

Afterword

My brothers and sisters, my friends, listen to me carefully. I teach you to have faith in the Most Beautiful and most Blessed Virgin Mary, your Divine Mother far beyond the confines of this book. Say the following with me:

Hail Mary, full of Grace, the Lord is with thee; blessed art thou among women and blessed is the fruit of thy womb, Jesus. Holy Mary, Mother of God, pray for us sinners, now and at the hour of our death. Amen. Behold the handmaid of the Lord: Be it done unto me according to Thy word.

I love you
Saint Bernadette

About the Author

Marie-Josée Thibault's life is in no way similar to yours. When she wakes, the saints of Heaven visit her, talk to her, teach her, and pray intensely with her. When such mystical sessions draw to a close, she greets with great respect and deep reverence the Masters of the Heavenly Court. This servant of the Lord spends the rest of the day in the company of her guardian angel, who continues her spiritual education and ceaselessly protects her from the perils of this fallen world.

Bestowed by the Heavenly Father, her gifts of clairvoyance and clairaudience allow her to remain in continuous contact with the supernatural dimension juxtaposed with ours, where the soul is born of the Spirit through Jesus and Mary. She prays that, one day soon, the entire human race will give glory to the Father, the Son, and the Holy Spirit.

Also by the Author

- Abba, Your Father, Speaks: Book I
- Abba, Your Father, Speaks: Book II
- Abba, Your Father, Speaks: Book III
- Abba, Your Father, Speaks: Book IV
- Dear Humanity: Book 1
- Dear Humanity: Book 2
- St Therese of Lisieux Speaks - Book 1: I Am The Heart of the Rose
- Saint Francis of Assisi Speaks - Book 1
- Saint Francis of Assisi Speaks - Book 2
- Saint Martin de Porres Speaks - Book 1
- Saint Bernadette Speaks - Book 1
- Saint Joan of Arc Speaks - Book 1
- Saint Padre Pio Speaks: Book 1
- Saint Beethoven Speaks - Book 1
- Saint Barnabas Speaks - Book 1
- Angel Gabriel Speaks: Book 1
- The Holy Pope Saint John Paul II Speaks - Book 1
- The Holy Pope Saint John Paul II Speaks - Book 2
- Prophet Moses Speaks 1
- Saint John the Baptist Speaks

www.ingramcontent.com/pod-product-compliance
Lightning Source LLC
Chambersburg PA
CBHW041430300426
44114CB00002B/20